*For Gabe and Luke*
M. C.


*For Frank and Jean*
J. S.

BENJAMIN'S BOX

published by Gold'n'Honey Books
*a part of the Questar publishing family*

© 1997 by Questar Publishers, Inc.

*International Standard Book Number: 1-57673-139-1*

Text by Melody Carlson

Illustration by Jack Stockman

Design by D2 DesignWorks

Printed in the United States of America


*Most Scripture quotations are from the New International Version*
*© 1973, 1984 by International Bible Society*
*used by permission of Zondervan Publishing House*

For information:
QUESTAR PUBLISHERS, INC.
POST OFFICE BOX 1720
SISTERS, OREGON 97759


98 99 00 01 — 10 9 8 7 6 5 4 3

A Resurrection Story

# BENJAMIN'S BOX

*Story by Melody Carlson*
*Illustrations by Jack Stockman*

FOREWORD BY BARBARA RAINEY

Gold 'n' Honey
BOOKS

SISTERS, OREGON

# FOREWORD

I believe that one of the finest tools for teaching spiritual truth is the family. God has entrusted moms and dads, grandmothers and grandfathers, aunts and uncles with the next generation. It is up to us to pass on a godly heritage and to be sure that our children have the biblical foundation necessary to withstand the many challenges found in today's world.

That's why I am so excited about using the memorable story of *Benjamin's Box* along with Resurrection Eggs® (FamilyLife's colorful eggs containing objects that illustrate key events in the death, burial, and Resurrection of Jesus Christ). As you share the fictional story of little Benjamin, the Easter story will come alive to the children you love.

Children will be captivated when items found in Resurrection Eggs are shown as *Benjamin's Box* is read. Their eyes will sparkle when they handle tangible objects while hearing of Benjamin's treasures: a piece of leather, a coin, a nail. And how powerful it will be to then turn to Scripture passages relating to Christ's crucifixion and Resurrection.

The Resurrection is the pivotal point in all of human history. The one thing that separates Christianity from other religions is that Jesus Christ conquered death. "He is not here. He has risen!" (Luke 24:6)

May God use *Benjamin's Box* and Resurrection Eggs as ministry tools to bring countless children into His eternal kingdom.

*Barbara Rainey*

Barbara Rainey is the wife of Dennis Rainey, executive director of FamilyLife. FamilyLife, a division of Campus Crusade for Christ, has been working to bring God's blueprints to marriages and families since 1976.

For more information on how to order Resurrection Eggs please call: 1-800-FL-TODAY

# HOW TO USE THIS BOOK WITH RESURRECTION EGGS®

hile *Benjamin's Box* can be enjoyed as a stand-alone story, it is designed to be used with FamilyLife's Resurrection Eggs. The goal of the book and Resurrection Eggs is to present the true story of Easter in a way that children can understand and remember. We also suggest you read what each Scripture says.

**1.** How Resurrection Eggs and *Benjamin's Box* complement each other: With color-coordinated eggs and symbols, *Benjamin's Box* helps you know exactly when a child should open the egg that pertains to that page of the story. It also ties in well to the booklet provided with Resurrection Eggs. Use these resources:

- in your home
- at your church
- with your neighbors

**2.** Creative ways to use Resurrection Eggs and *Benjamin's Box*: Here are two ways to create a fun time for all.

*Use Resurrection Eggs in a traditional egg hunt.* Tell the children not to open the eggs until everyone comes back together. After the children have found all the eggs, read *Benjamin's Box*, inviting the children to open the corresponding egg as it appears in the book.

*After you have hidden Resurrection Eggs, read* Benjamin's Box *aloud.* After the story is finished, the children can search for the eggs and open them as they find them. Invite the children to share what they thought of when they opened the eggs and ask them if they have any questions. Use the booklet from Resurrection Eggs as a reference to ensure the children understand the Gospel thoroughly.

# BENJAMIN

Long ago, in the faraway land of Palestine, there lived a boy named Benjamin. His small humble home was nestled into a wall of other houses, almost hidden on a narrow back street in the bustling city of Jerusalem. Benjamin loved Jerusalem because God's temple was there. More than that, Benjamin loved God! His grandfather had taught him many things about God when he was just a tiny boy.

Benjamin talked to God a lot. He whispered prayers each night at sunset. And in the morning, he always gave thanks for the new day.

Benjamin's parents worked hard weaving and selling cloth, but their family was still quite poor. So Benjamin helped out by taking odd jobs around the city. Everyone in Jerusalem seemed to know Benjamin. They could always count on him to be honest and work hard.

# THE BOX

ne bright spring morning, Benjamin sat outside in the sunshine. In his hands was a wooden box.

"Hi, Benjamin," called his friend, Eli. "What's that you've got?"

"It's my treasure box," said Benjamin. "My grandfather gave it to me before he died last year. He said it was very, very special."

Eli opened it and looked in. "There's nothing in it except for some old straw. How can this be a treasure box?"

Benjamin shrugged. "I don't have any real treasures yet. But my grandfather said this straw came from the bed of a baby who was born in a stable. My grandfather was a shepherd then, and he said the baby would grow up to be a king."

"Why would a king be born in a stable with cows and donkeys?" Eli laughed and closed the box. "I heard some sort of king is coming today. His name is Jesus. Want to come to the city gate and watch for him?"

"Sure. My grandfather took me to hear a man called Jesus once. I liked to listen to him!"

# THE DONKEY

MATTHEW 21: 1-9

Crowds were already lining the street. Some people cut palm branches from trees and handed them around. Others laid garments on the street like a carpet.

"Wow!" said Benjamin. "He must be a king!" The two boys squeezed through the throng just as a donkey entered the gate. "That's him!" Benjamin pointed to the man on the donkey. "That's Jesus!" "Hosanna, Hosanna!" cheered the crowd as they waved their palm branches in the air.

"Hail to our new king!" yelled an old man beside Benjamin.

"Why does a king ride an ordinary donkey?" asked Benjamin.

The old man turned. "It means he comes in peace. Jesus has come to set us free! Hail, King Jesus!"

Benjamin looked into Jesus' face as he drew near. Jesus smiled back — as if they were friends! The donkey plodded along and Benjamin followed, pushing through the crowd to keep up. At last, he drew close enough to pet the donkey. A small tuft of hair came off in his hand.

That night Benjamin placed the bit of donkey fur in his treasure box.

# THE COIN

MATTHEW 26:14-15, 46-50, 27: 1-5

In the next days, Benjamin and Eli went to hear Jesus whenever they could. One day as they waited, Eli whispered, "The priests have offered money for someone to betray Jesus."

"Why?" asked Benjamin. "What has he done? He only speaks the truth. They should listen to him."

"The priests are jealous of him. They want Jesus to stop teaching," said Eli.

"Someone should warn Jesus," declared Benjamin. "I'm not afraid. I'll go." He pushed through the crowd until he reached one of Jesus' friends. He tugged on the man's sleeve.

"Excuse me, sir? Are you with Jesus?"

"Yes, I am," the man answered.

"Please, I need to warn Jesus. He's in danger, the priests are offering a bribe to betray him! You must tell—"

"Shh," said the man. "Do not repeat this. I'll take care of it." And he slipped a coin into Benjamin's hand.

"Thank you, kind sir. What is your name?"

"Judas Iscariot," said the man as he turned away.

That night, Benjamin tucked the shiny denarius into his treasure box.

# THE CUP

MATTHEW 26:17-19, 26-28

he next day, Benjamin was asked to help his aunt get ready for unexpected guests. They would be coming for Passover dinner. He went right to work carrying water jugs.

"Did you hear the guest of honor is Jesus?" said a servant girl.

Benjamin's eyes opened wide. Imagine — to serve such an important man! He must work hard and do his very best.

Two of Jesus' friends came to help, and Benjamin listened as they talked of Jesus. They loved him so much!

Soon Jesus arrived, and the supper began. If Benjamin listened carefully he could hear some of their words. But what did Jesus mean when he said the wine was like his blood and would be spilled, and the bread was to be broken like his body. It made no sense.

Then Jesus said someone would betray him. Benjamin smiled, he wasn't worried. He knew that Judas would prevent this.

After supper, Benjamin found a broken cup. He saved it to remember the night when he served Jesus.

# PRAYING HANDS

MARK 14:32-42

ater, Jesus and his friends left to pray. Benjamin wanted to pray too. He followed at a distance, watching as they finally stopped in a garden. Benjamin sat beneath an olive tree and broke off a twig. He couldn't hear Jesus, but he knew he was praying.

Benjamin prayed too. And as he prayed he rubbed the twig between his hands. Before long, his eyelids grew heavy and he soon fell asleep.

Loud yelling startled Benjamin. He leaped up in time to see soldiers taking Jesus away. "Stop!" he cried. "You can't take him. He hasn't done anything—"

"Shh, boy!" said one of Jesus' friends, holding Benjamin back.

"What's wrong?" demanded Benjamin. "Why are they taking him?"

"They want to question him."

Benjamin pulled away. "Why didn't you stop them?" But the man just shook his head and walked away. All Jesus' friends were gone now.

Benjamin saw the smooth twig in his hand. "Dear God, please take care of my friend, Jesus," he prayed as he walked. At home, he placed the broken cup and the twig in his box.

# THE LEATHER STRIP

JOHN 19:1-15

**B**enjamin, did you hear the news?" asked Eli the next morning. "They've locked Jesus up. Everyone says that Judas Iscariot got a bunch of money to betray him."

Benjamin gasped. He had told Judas about the bribe — maybe this was his fault! He said good-bye to Eli and wandered through the city. What could he do? Was there any way to help? Sounds of shouting made him stop, and he turned to see an angry crowd.

"Jesus deserved that beating!" snarled an old man. "That heretic claims to be God's son!"

"He should be stoned!" yelled another, shaking a fist.

"What's going on?" asked Benjamin. "Did they hurt Jesus?"

"What do you know about this Jesus?" demanded the old man. They all turned and stared at Benjamin with angry eyes.

"No— nothing," he stammered. His gaze dropped to the ground where he noticed a small strip of leather. He picked it up. It was from the whips used by soldiers. It was wet with blood. He tucked it in his tunic and slipped away. Why would anyone beat Jesus?

# THE THORN

MATTHEW 27:29

**B**enjamin continued to walk. If only he could make them release Jesus. But what could a small boy do? He heard loud cries as another crowd gathered at the end of the street.

"Hail, King of the Jews!" yelled a soldier as Benjamin pushed his way past men and women.

And there stood Jesus.

Benjamin looked into Jesus' eyes as Roman soldiers threw a shabby robe over his beaten back. He expected to see hatred, but instead saw only love. Just then a soldier shoved a crown of thorns onto Jesus' head. And another struck him with a stick.

Benjamin's eyes filled with tears. Why were they doing this? A few days ago, everyone had called Jesus a king when he entered Jerusalem. Now it seemed they all hated him. Benjamin squatted down and buried his head in his hands. "Please, God," he prayed over and over. "Please, make them stop!" When he finally opened his eyes, the crowd had moved along. Jesus was gone. He walked over to where they had scorned his friend and picked up a sharp thorn broken from the awful crown.

He ran home. His parents paused to hear his story, then sadly shook their heads and returned to their work. Benjamin placed the thorn and leather strip in his box and cried.

# THE NAIL

JOHN 19:16-22

**B**enjamin!" called Eli. "Have you heard? Jesus is to be crucified!"

"No!" cried Benjamin. "He has done nothing to deserve that!"

Eli frowned. "My father says that only the worst criminals are put to death on a cross."

Benjamin went inside and sat in a dark corner of his house. He did not want to talk, or even to think about this sad news. But in his mind he could still see the evil men hurting Jesus.

"I must go!" he finally said aloud. "If this is partly my fault, I can at least be there. I can pray for him."

"Where are you going?" asked his mother as he opened the door.

"To help a friend," he said. She nodded and touched his cheek.

As Benjamin climbed the hill, he found a large spike. It was like those used by Romans to nail criminals to crosses. He tucked it in his tunic and continued on. Three crosses stood at the top. But he could not force his eyes to look upon his friend.

He noticed a small group of people apart from the larger crowd. He knew they were Jesus' dearest friends. He sat near them and bowed to pray. But the only words that came were, "I'm sorry, God. I'm so sorry. . ."

# THE DIE & THE SPEAR

JOHN 19:23-25, 32-34

**B**enjamin watched as soldiers gambled for Jesus' clothes. He tried to shut his ears to their cruel remarks.

Finally, he forced himself to look up. Benjamin looked into Jesus' eyes and saw such sorrow and pain that it cut to his heart. But he also saw love. And like before, Jesus looked right at Benjamin. Surely, this was his way of saying all would be well. Perhaps he would even do a miracle!

But instead the sky turned dark and Jesus cried out, "Father, into your hands I commit my spirit!" The ground shook, and Jesus breathed his last breath. Benjamin was stunned.

Jesus was dead!

As if in a dream, Benjamin heard the people move about. He saw a soldier pierce his friend's side with a spear. People hurried to take down crosses and bodies before the Sabbath began. Soon they were gone, and he was alone. He picked up a stone the soldiers had gambled with and looked up at the dark sky. Why had God allowed it?

Later that night, he opened his treasure box and placed the nail and the gambling stone inside. He looked at his collection. It had seemed so valuable when he believed Jesus was the King. But now the strange items only filled him with unbearable sadness.

# THE CLOTH

MATTHEW 27:57-61

**B**enjamin!" called Eli the next morning. "Come hear the news!" Benjamin stuck his head out the window and rubbed his sleepy eyes.

"They posted guards at Jesus' tomb," explained Eli. "Some say that Jesus will return to life!"

Benjamin perked up. "My Grandfather told me that Jesus brought some people back from the dead."

"Maybe it will happen again!" said Eli. "But the soldiers say they're making sure people don't steal the body." Quickly, Benjamin dressed and raced to the tomb. Could it be? Could Jesus have returned to life? How he hoped so!

But the huge stone remained in place and the guards blocked the tomb. With dark scowling faces, they told him to leave at once. As Benjamin walked slowly down the hill, he noticed a bit of white cloth hanging from a small branch. He plucked it off and rubbed it between his fingers. His parents wove cloth like this for burials.

"Jesus is dead," he told himself as he continued toward home.

That night he sadly placed the cloth in his box. This would surely be the last thing to remember his friend by. He tried to pray, but no words came. He wondered if God even listened.

# THE STONE

MATTHEW 28:1-2

arly the next morning, Benjamin went to the market for his mother. He used to enjoy the crowds in the city, but now they only reminded him of how everyone had turned against Jesus. He shuffled along without looking up.

"It's a miracle!" shrieked a girl. Benjamin stopped in his tracks and listened. "Jesus has risen from the dead! The stone's been moved!"

Benjamin turned and ran from the market and up toward the tomb. Could it possibly be true? Could Jesus have risen from the grave? In his heart he believed it could be. It must be! He ran even faster.

Sure enough, the stone was rolled away! He fell to his knees and thanked God. When he stood, he picked up a sharp piece of broken rock. It must have crumbled from the huge stone.

With a joyful heart he marched back down to town. Jesus was alive!

In the market, he met a woman who was a friend of Jesus. "I know the good news," he said. "Jesus is alive!"

"Yes!" She smiled. "It's as the prophet said, 'On the third day He'll rise.' Some of us have even seen him!"

Benjamin ran home and told his parents. He placed the stone in the box. What a treasure he had now!

# HE IS RISEN!

MATTHEW 28:5-8

D uring the next few days, Benjamin and Eli listened as the disciples shared about how Jesus had appeared to them in various places.

"Jesus said that all this came to pass just so forgiveness could be preached to all nations — beginning right here in Jerusalem," explained a disciple. "He said that since we saw all these things, now we can go out to tell others the good news of His forgiveness!"

Benjamin smiled. Now he understood that Jesus had forgiven him too. And he wanted to share the good news. He ran home and got his treasure box, and went out into the streets and gathered all of his friends.

"Inside this box," he explained, "is a great treasure."

The children drew closer and listened with excitement.

One by one, Benjamin took out each item. He explained how he got it, and what it all meant.

"And so you see," he said as he closed the box and looked into their faces. *"The treasure is really Jesus!* Because of what Jesus did on the cross, we can all be forgiven by God the Father!"

They all cheered and begged him to tell the story again!

# THANK YOU

hat night Benjamin opened his box one more time before he went to bed. He examined each item, handling them all with love and care. Finally he placed the last one back in the box. Then he knelt and prayed.

"Dear God, thank you for letting me find all these special treasures. But most of all, I thank you for sending me the greatest treasure of all. Thank you for sending Jesus. And help me to be a good servant for Jesus. Help me to tell everyone I know about the good news! Amen."

Jesus said, "I'll tell you the truth,

unless you change and become like little children,

you will never enter the kingdom of heaven.

Therefore, whoever humbles himself like this child

is the greatest in the kingdom, of heaven.

And whoever welcomes a little child

like this in my name welcomes me."

MATTHEW 18: 2-5

# FAMILYLIFE'S TEN TIPS TO LEADING CHILDREN TO CHRIST

*1. Make a friend.* Children need to feel comfortable discussing spiritual issues. It's important for them to understand that your reason for sharing is because you love and care about them.

*2. Keep it simple.* The biggest mistake adults make is over-complicating the gospel. Remember to think like children. Speak their language.

*3. Let them share.* Give children a chance to tell how they feel or what concerns them. The more you understand them, the better you can share.

*4. Mention Jesus.* Ask them who they think Jesus is. Then explain that He was not just a man, nor was He just God. But because He is both God and man, he could be perfect and yet still die a human death to pay for our sin.

*5. Use visual aids.* Like with this book and the Resurrection Eggs the gospel comes to life for children when they see or experience something tangible.

*6. Invite a decision.* Explain how they can have a personal relationship with Jesus. Be sensitive. Is it God's timing for them to make this commitment?

*7. Pray with them.* Again, keep it simple. If they like, they can repeat after you: a) I believe that Jesus is God, and He died on the cross for my sin, b) I want to change, c) please forgive me for my sin, d) thank you, Jesus, for forgiving me, and e) Holy Spirit, please teach and help me to obey God.

*8. Encourage them.* Share with them about how all of heaven is rejoicing over their new relationship with Jesus. Show them how excited you are. Tell them that although being a Christian can be hard, God has sent the Holy Spirit to help them.

*9. Give them homework.* Share ways they can grow (Bible, prayer, fellowship). Make sure they have an easy-to-read Bible available.

*10. Tell them to tell others.* Encourage them to share their new commitment to Jesus by telling friends and family. This helps solidify their decision.